Light Gathering At The Edge

The Edge

Reflections from the Quiet Ground

Anne Hester Neumann

/ BookLeaf
Publishing

India | USA | UK

Made with ❤ on the BookLeaf Publishing Platform
www.bookleafpub.in
www.bookleafpub.com

Dedication

For the quiet wanderers, on foot and in thought.

Preface

This collection is a tracing of quiet moments: the cool touch of morning grass, the soft weight of stillness, the fleeting light that gathers at the edge of day. I write as one who wanders—through thought, memory, and the world around me—seeking the small, overlooked spaces where life quietly speaks.

These poems are an invitation to pause, to notice, and to linger, even for a moment, in the gentle presence of what is.

Acknowledgements

I am grateful to the quiet mornings, the damp grass beneath my feet, and the soft light that gathers at the edges of day.

Thank you to my family and friends, whose encouragement and presence have carried me through moments of doubt and kept my curiosity alive. To the fleeting thoughts, the small wonders of the world, and the spaces of stillness that stirred these poems into being —your influence lingers in every line.

And to the landscapes, the seasons, and the gentle rhythms of life that held me steady, I offer my gratitude for guiding these words into existence.

1. Morning Light

I pause at the doorway,
seeing myself in the mirror—
a face both familiar and changed.
Time has softened edges,
etched quiet stories into my skin,
and in every line
I trace the life I have lived.
The cool, damp grass greets my feet,
the world still and hushed,
wrapped in darkness,
breathing with me,
holding a quiet promise.
I linger,
feeling the weight of all that has shaped me—
losses, loves,
dreams that called my name,
lessons learned in silence,
the gentle shaping of seasons.
Every step, every moment,
woven into the self I now behold.
The horizon begins to soften,
light spilling slowly,
touching the edges of the night.

And I wonder,
heart open and still—
am I waiting for the light,
or has the light
been waiting for me
all along?

2. The Quiet Between

This morning, I stood in the cool earth,
 feet pressed into the damp grass,
 eyes lifted to the sky.
The sun rose softly in the East,
 gold spilling across the horizon,
 while in the West, a storm gathered,
 dark clouds rolling, restless and heavy.
I felt both at once—
 light and shadow, warmth and weight,
 reminders that each day carries both joy and challenge.
Both teach me to breathe, to notice,
 to move with patience and courage.
 Both guide me toward resilience.

3. Take The Bumpy Road

The grass—
cool, damp beneath my feet,
dew clinging like tiny jewels
left from night.
The sky softens—
rose and gold spilling
into pale blue,
pushing back the shadows.
The earth rises in ridges and bumps,
pressing into my soles,
steadying me.
Soil smells of life—
rich, loamy, alive—
carrying me backward through time.
I am small again,
climbing into my father's black Studebaker.
The door is heavy in my hands,
the cab smells of dust and oil, of warmth.
"Take the bumpy road, Dad," I whisper,
voice trembling with anticipation.
He smiles—patient, knowing—
and the truck lurches onto the rough path.
Ruts and hollows throw me against the seat,
my stomach flips—fear and joy entangled.

Silent laughter rises,
caught in a rhythm I did not yet know
would follow me through life.
Now, morning light pours across the damp grass.
The same pulse runs beneath my feet.
The bumps, the uneven ground, the living earth—
all speak of a life imperfect, full, awake.
And the child inside me whispers still—
eyes bright, heart racing:
Take the bumpy road, Dad—
take it again.

4. Waking to Thunder

Morning opens with a flash—
lightning stitching the edge of the sky,
thunder rolling low and steady
like an old memory stirring awake.
I am carried back to childhood,
to nights when storms
felt vast and untamed,
when the world cracked open
and wonder felt close to fear.
Now, I listen differently.
The rhythm is familiar—
a heartbeat,
a pulse in the air.
Rain begins to fall,
each drop a quiet drumbeat
against the waiting earth.
There's beauty in this wildness,
a kind of peace
that only comes
when we stop resisting the storm
and let it pass through us—
light, sound,
and stillness intertwined.

5. The Quiet Of Wings

A single white feather lay in the grass—
soft, still,
as if it had been placed there
for me to notice.
Above, the stars lingered,
fading slowly
into the pale light of dawn,
a quiet signal of a new day.
Yesterday, I watched the birds take flight—
each moving alone,
yet circling together in a graceful rhythm,
a silent dance of wings,
a reminder of the strength and beauty
that comes from moving together.
The feather speaks differently—
pause, presence, stillness,
the gift of simply being.
I carry both with me today—
the memory of the flock's motion,
the quiet of the feather,

6. Closer Than They Appear

Barefoot in dew,
I step into the gray morning—
a quiet pause
between yesterday
and whatever comes next.
Yesterday's photo
flashes behind my eyes:
a pickup mirror
catching the road behind me,
cars trailing like thoughts
I thought I had left behind.
The sun breaks through clouds
in soft streaks of orange and gold,
a gentle reminder
that hope travels quietly
even through grayness.
Across the glass,
words linger:
"Objects in mirror are closer than they appear."
And I feel it—
how memories ride with us,
how moments, people, light
fold into the paths we walk,
always nearer than they seem.

Here, in the stillness,
I am suspended
between what was and what is,
breathing in the closeness of it all—
past, present, road ahead,
and the quiet wonder
of being alive in the middle.

7. The Unseen Still Holds

The morning met me in the cut grass,
cool blades pressing against my skin,
the earth beneath sure and solid—
a grounding I didn't know I needed.
Above, the clouds gathered thick and gray,
muting the sun's bright voice.
And I thought—
how often life feels just like this,
the light still burning somewhere,
but hidden from view.
A breeze passed through,
soft as breath against my cheek.
I couldn't see it,
but I knew it by the way it touched me,
the way it reminded me
that the unseen is still real,
still moving, still near.
So I stayed a little longer,
breathing in the quiet proof
that not all knowing comes through sight.
Faith lives in the feel of the air,
in the whisper between heartbeats,
in the steady promise

that life holds me—
even when I can't yet see the light.

8. Hands In the Moonlight

I step outside,
cold brushing my skin,
but my hands draw me in.
I lift them to the moonlight,
and simply watch.
Every line, every crease, every scar
is a map of all they've carried —
the work, the worry,
the tenderness, the grief.
I flex them slowly,
feeling subtle warmth hum beneath the skin.
Quiet strength, steady and true,
the kind that doesn't announce itself.
These hands have built and repaired,
held and released,
comforted and defended.
They have shaken and steadied,
lifted and let go,
over and over again.
I trace the memory of their movements —
the gentle touch that soothed,
the firm grip that protected,
the soft patience that endured.

They know fear and courage,
heaviness and light.
Even in the cold,
even in the stillness,
I feel them pulse with life.
Strength lives quietly here —
in persistence, in tenderness,
in the act of showing up.
Under the bright full moon,
I honor them fully.
These hands —
and the life they hold —
are enough.

9. What the Morning Said

The clouds were slow-moving, deliberate,
and the moon slipped among them—
a shy traveler,
unsure whether to stay or go.
The ground was soft and warm,
as if the night had left
a parting kindness.
The air did not stir.
Even the trees stood listening.
Somewhere, a cricket sang—
a small, steadfast sound,
carrying more patience
than I seem to find in myself.
I thought then
of how quietly the world remakes itself,
how each small shift—
a change in light,
a breath of warmth—
is the beginning of something new.
And I understood:
peace is not the stillness of things,
but the willingness

to meet their turning
with an open heart.

10. Bare Feet, Steady Earth

This morning I opened the door
 and stepped into the yard —
 cool, wet grass slipping between my toes,
 waking me more than any cup of coffee could.
The blades are already changing,
 browns threading through the green.
 I pause, breathing in crisp air,
 the kind that clears fog from the mind.
Something in these quiet steps
 slows the world down.
 The damp earth reminds me
 I am held by something ancient,
 something steady.
In that stillness, I think
 how we, too, are connected —
 each of us wishing
 to be seen,
 to be heard,
 to know we matter.
Standing barefoot in morning grass,
 I feel that truth settle in:
 the world moving fast around me,

but here — breath, body,
shifting season,
and the steady earth
all aligned.

11. A Letter to My Younger Self

This morning, the yard was still —
the kind of quiet that feels alive,
that waits with you.
The grass was cool and damp,
pressing against my feet,
each step reminding me
that the world holds steady
even when I do not.
The air smelled of earth and leaf,
the tender edge of fall —
a season teaching me
that letting go can be gentle.
Dear younger me,
I think of you in mornings like this,
when nothing needs to be said,
when the light hasn't yet made up its mind.
You wanted so much to be sure,
to have the map,
to walk without trembling.
But here's what I've learned:
the trembling *is* the way.
It means you are alive,
it means the heart is awake.

You thought strength was something to prove.
Now I know it is something to listen for —
a quiet pulse under the noise,
a steady breath that says: stay.
I wish you could see
how your wondering became prayer,
how your uncertainty grew into grace.
So I stand here in the cool morning light,
barefoot and breathing,
and whisper through the years —
thank you
for your questions,
for your courage,
for beginning the walk

12. What Is Rising

I stepped out later than usual,
the morning already unfolding —
the sun a soft ache behind gray clouds.

The wind was full of itself,
pushing through the trees,
calling the loose leaves to follow.

Two turkey vultures lifted into the current,
dark sails steady against the restless air.
They did not resist.
They rose because the wind rose.

I stood there watching,
feeling that same invisible pull —
something unnamed
beginning to move inside me.

Change rarely arrives with fanfare.
It comes like this —
in the gray between light and storm,
in the steady wings of what trusts the air.

13. What the Breath Carries

I step outside.
Fall spills over the world —
crisp air filling my lungs,
damp earth pressing softly beneath my feet,
leaves turning gold and russet,
whispering in the wind.
My breath moves quietly,
unseen,
threading through the grass,
curling around the trunks of trees,
dancing with the drifting leaves,
tangling with the distant song of birds,
blending with the slow, steady turning of the season.
Each inhale gathers the morning,
the scent of soil and moss,
the faint sweetness of fallen leaves,
the hush of light through branches.
Each exhale lets go of what I no longer need —
tension, lingering thought, shadow —
stretching outward
into the air, into the earth, into everything.
I pause.
The ground is soft in some places, firm in others.

A golden beam of sunlight brushes a leaf;
the wind shifts, carrying a quiet music.
I am held in it all,
my breath weaving me into the living pulse
of this world,
of this moment,
of fall itself.

14. Where Silence Speaks

The grass is cool beneath my feet,
each blade carrying
the damp scent of fall—
the slow decay of leaves,
the rich hum of earth
turning toward rest.
Above, the moon hangs pale
and steady in the deep morning sky,
watching without sound.
When everything stops speaking,
the world reveals its quiet music:
roots stretching through soil,
leaves brushing against one another
in secret conversations,
the faint stir of creatures
waking in hidden places.
In that vast, tender hum
we are small,
and yet fully part of everything:
each breath, each movement, each thought
woven into the same rhythm
that carries rivers, stones, trees, sky.

Even silence is alive.
Even stillness

15. The Watching Moon

The rain has been falling since before dawn—
soft, steady, almost shy.
The air feels close and kind,
the kind of morning that invites you to listen.
I look up,
but the moon is hidden.
Still, I know she is there,
somewhere above the clouds,
keeping her quiet vigil.
How faithful the unseen things are—
the roots working in the dark,
the seeds waiting beneath the surface,
the light folded gently into shadow.
Love moves like that too—
unseen, but constant.
The world feels tender in its persistence.
Every drop of rain,
every breath of wind,
reminds me that even what's hidden
is still alive.
I stand in the gray morning,

letting the rain find my hands,
and whisper thank you

16. Almost Missed, Yet Given

The morning is hushed,
a soft gray draped across the yard.
The grass cools my feet,
the scent of rain still lingering in the air.
Nothing stirs—
until a faint movement near the hedges,
a rabbit, quiet as breath,
pausing just long enough
for me to notice.
I almost miss it—
that tender exchange
between seeing and being seen.
It feels like the echo of a kind word,
not loud,
but steady,
carrying warmth into the silence.
When it slips away,
the stillness returns—
only now it hums differently,
as if touched by something gentle.
And I wonder how many moments like this

go unseen,
how many kindnesses
pass through the world
without needing to be known,

17. Just Before First Light

The grass is damp beneath my feet,
cool and quiet.
Darkness surrounds me—
familiar, still—
carrying memories I hadn't touched in years:
faces, voices,
small vanished moments
that drift in softly,
as if remembering me, too.
Every sound feels sharper:
a leaf moves,
a branch shifts,
the faint stir of wind.
The night waits patiently,
letting the past rise
and settle again,
without demand or haste.
Somewhere beyond this darkness
morning gathers—
I cannot see it yet,
the horizon unbroken,
the sky still closed.
Yet the air carries promise,

a quiet readiness—
the tender assurance
that light will come.
And I stand here,
in shadow and in memory,
feeling both the weight of night
and the soft, certain hope

18. The Kindness of the Body

I feel you under my skin,
soft and steady.
Through long nights, through days that ache,
you carry me.
You have known illness,
and worry,
and the endless demands of labor.
You have borne new life
and found the quiet repair afterward.
I notice the cost now:
the fatigue tucked into my bones,
the small tremors I pretend not to see.
And still, you rise.
Still, you offer breath.
Still, you offer balance, life.
This morning, you are like the moon,
showing only a sliver of your light,
yet holding the rest
within.
I touch you,
I honor you.

This body—
tender, tireless—
rises with the light once more

19. Conversation with the Season

I step outside and let the world speak—
the crisp air, the tilted sun,
the soft decay of leaves underfoot.
Each thing is a sentence,
a whisper I almost remember.
The season says: *Slow down.*
Notice the edges where change begins.
And I answer: *I am listening.*
I will honor the pause, the turning.
It says: *Release what no longer serves you,*
like the trees shedding their leaves.
And I answer: *I let go, with tenderness,*
trusting that what falls will feed what comes next.
It says: *There is beauty even in endings.*
And I answer: *I see it, even when it stings.*
I breathe it in and carry it with me.
The conversation unfolds quietly.
No need for words—
only presence.
The world outside mirrors what is within,
and I learn again

how to be both open and still,
like the season itself.

20. The Weight of Memory

Darkness holds the world.
A few stars remain,
faint sparks in the fading night.
The wind moves across my face,
cool and familiar,
a gentle reminder that I am here,
that the earth breathes beneath my feet.
Memory rises from the soil,
from the pulse of leaves,
from the spaces between heartbeats—
not polished, not meant for telling,
but alive in the body,
in the soft ache of something once loved.
I lift it gently,
like a stone found in shadow,
and ask nothing.
It rests there with me.
The house waits ahead,
its windows soft with light.
I return toward it,
carrying the tender weight

21. At the Edges of Light

I have walked
through quiet and bright seasons,
through loss and small graces.
Each step left something behind—
patience pressed in my hands,
tenderness tucked into my chest,
the rhythm of beginning again.
Now I stand
where the air opens wide,
where light gathers
on the treetops
and in the hollows of me.
It comes softly,
without hurry,
reminding me
I am still here,
still becoming.
I carry
the courage to show up,
the joy in small things,
the gratitude for a world
that keeps unfolding.
I offer back

a smile,
a listening heart,
a quiet faith

www.ingramcontent.com/pod-product-compliance
Lightning Source LLC
Chambersburg PA
CBHW050950030426
42339CB00007B/374